the Power of Words

Life is on the tongue...

by

Mark A. Thomas

THP
THE HOUSE PUBLICATIONS

The Power of Words
Life is on the tongue

ISBN 1-932997-00-8

Copyright © 2004 by Mark A. Thomas
Mark A. Thomas Ministries, Inc.
P.O. Box 6339
Corona, CA 92878

Published by The House Publications, Inc.
Corona, California USA.

the *Power* of **Words**

Life is on the tongue...

Contents

~6~

Personal Message...

W hat I am about to share with you will change your life today. It has changed my life and the lives of many others that have practiced these same principles. If you are reading this, the process of change for you has already begun and will continue as you read, pause, meditate, and take a deep breath in-between these chapters. I've included some blank pages at the back of the book where you can write notes, so that you may use them as a reference from time to time. So grab a pen and take some notes for yourself.

In the summer of 1994, I made a quality decision to take God at His Word and began speaking what He had already said about my life. I'd heard other great men and women of God say over and over again, speak God's Word and it will soon manifest in your life. Well, I said, "Yeah right...that works for you. It's easy for you to say that, you're on TV."

If I go any further telling that story, I'd have to call this book something else. Let me say this, I stood on One Confession while my wife and I were living in someone else's house on $400 per month income with 2 kids. Today the secret behind the Power of Words, that I have learned and experienced, must be shared; so that other believers can be changed and set free from any area of lack - physically, spiritually, and financially. Today, I can say with a pure heart, that I am debt free because of God's Word.

Lay aside whatever problems, worries, or burdens that you may have in your heart, and let the Holy Spirit escort you into His place of peace and prosperity for your life. It is His desire for you. All you have to do is be willing to change the way you speak – and I will show you how.

In Love,
Pastor Mark

Introduction

Too many people misinterpret the *authority* behind the **Power of Words**. You take for granted the fact that you are created in the image of God and in His authority. When you are dealing with the power of words, you have to realize that God's Word works. What you say is what you get, and what you confess is what you possess. Your confession of the Word precedes your possession of God's promises.

Did you know that the average Christian spends only 1 hour a week in church? With such limited exposure to the Word of God, you cannot expect to gain enough understanding to be able to see the Word work in your life. The Word says that faith comes by hearing and hearing by the Word of God, and without faith you cannot please God. So how can you please God, if you are only getting the Word of God 4 hours a month? You must come to the conclusion that you have to spend more time hearing the Word of God. The key is to hear the Word of God enough, so that its effects can manifest in your life. You need to understand that applying the Word of God must follow hearing the Word of God. Until you apply the principles of the Word of God, you will not see God's Word really working in your life.

Chapter 1

Words Carry Power

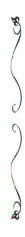

"Words kill, words give life; they're either poison or fruit — you choose.

Proverbs 18:21 MESSAGE

C h a p t e r 1

Words Carry Power

Words are Spiritual & Words Carry Power

Faith Pressure Applied to the Word of God

Confessions for Healing, Weakness, and Fear

Chapter 1

Words Carry Power

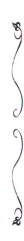

In order to get an understanding of how the power of words works, there are some important principles that you need to grasp. The following are two important principles about words:

1. __Words are spiritual.__

Every word that comes out of your mouth has an effect on something. Why? Because you are created in the image of God and you are a spirit being. Every word that comes out of the mouth of a spirit being is spiritual. (Genesis 1:26)

2. <u>Words carry power.</u>

Words carry one of two types of power. They carry the power of: 1) death or 2) life. God's Word coming out of your mouth produces exactly what He says.

The first thing you have to understand about these two principles is that you are created in God's image; and like God, what you say will come to pass. People say things all the time, over and over again, until they develop a habit of doubtful speech or conversation. We take the word "joke" as if it is a joke; but in reality, everything we say is eventually going to take place. It is not a question of **if** it will, but a matter of **when** it will. Your words are spiritual and they will produce. What you say may not be instantly manifested, but it is instantly processed. It is going out of your mouth working somewhere. God's Word produces exactly what He says.

If He does not say anything, then nothing happens.

He is not a God that said something in the Old Covenant that did not take place in the New Covenant. He is not a God that said something in the New Covenant that did not take place in our lives. All that He has said, every Word that has come out of His mouth, has taken place and has happened. (Psalm 89:34) That is why the enemy is always after our souls. He wants our souls so that he can get our expressions. If he gets our expressions, he gets a creative force of power, that power which is in natural spirits who have been born again in Christ Jesus.

The second thing you have to understand about these two principles is God's method of operation never changes. His creative force never changes. In other words, God is the same yesterday, today, and forever. Let us take a look at Deuteronomy 30:19 and Proverbs 18:21.

Deuteronomy 30:19 – King James Version
I call heaven and earth to record this day
against you, that I have set before you life
and death, blessing and cursing: therefore
choose life, that both thou and thy seed
may live:

In Deuteronomy 30:19, the Word of God says therefore choose life. Death is an area of lack, insufficiency, poverty, and curses. The word "Life" in the *Greek* language is pronounced "Zoe", which means the abundant life. The Word says choose life.

In Proverbs 18:21, we see clearly that our position today is a function of having the Word of God in our mouths, plus an understanding of the vital importance of the Word being there for us to use. The word to focus on is "indulge". The word "indulge" means *to do consistently*. You must have the Word of God in your mouth consistently, until you get fat on it, until you absorb everything that you can receive. You want to absorb it to the point that it becomes a part of your regular dialogue and a part of your everyday thinking. The Word says that you will eat the fruit of whatever you indulge in, whether it be death or life.

All of this is controlled by what comes out of our mouths. So when the Word comes out of our mouths, we are speaking life, and life has to manifest. There is a connection between your faith and the words you speak; we will explore that relationship next. For now, it is most important that you understand and conclude that words are spiritual, and death and life are in the power of your mouth. Death and life are, in other words, located in your mouth.

Let's look at Matthew…

Matthew 12:36-37 – Amplified
But I tell you, on the day of judgment men will have to give account for every idle (inoperative, nonworking) word they speak. For by your words you will be justified and

acquitted and by your words you will be condemned and sentenced.

The Amplified Bible describes idle words as inoperative or non-working. These are words that are not producing, because they are the result of carnal thinking. If you are believing God for a miracle and it is not working, your belief is based on words which do not line up with the Word of God. God's Word is the only *word* that does not return void.

The key to tapping into the power of words is to get God's Word in your mouth and in your heart. You cannot do this in merely 4 hours a month, a few days a year, and expect it to work. It will not be effective that way. The Word of God does not run on past experiences, faith is now. In other words, faith deals with the Word of God that is coming out of your mouth today, consistently, over and over again. It will have side effects on your life causing things to change around you, as well as in you.

Words played a vital role in what God has created. Over 10 different times, the Bible says that God said, and then God saw what He said. We are created in that same image and in His same likeness; we must realize that we are spirit beings and not just human beings. As a spirit being, you produce the same way God produces – with your mouth. Here is what Hebrews 11:1-3 say about the matter.

Hebrews 11:1-3 – King James Version
Now faith is the substance of things hoped for, the evidence of things not seen.
For by it the elders obtained a good report. Through faith we understand that the worlds were framed by the word of God, so that things which are seen were not made of things which do appear.

Hebrews 11:1 – Amplified
Now Faith is the assurance (the confirmation, the title deed) of the things [we] hope for, being the proof of things

[we] do not see and the conviction of their reality [faith perceiving as real fact what is not revealed to the senses].

The Amplified Bible says that faith is your confidence in the Word of God. It is your confirmation of the Word of God. You cannot somehow gain confidence in the Word if you are not hearing the Word. Confidence comes by hearing. Faith is the necessary substance that is required to make God's Word work when you speak it. If you are speaking lack, insufficiency, or pridefulness, God's promises cannot come to pass. Pridefulness makes us blame our current circumstances on our past experiences. There is no need for that. We are not in the past. You are a new creature in Christ Jesus. All old things have passed away and behold all things are now new, even your words!

Faith is the confidence in, or the confirmation of, things you do not see. As you get more of God's Word coming out of your mouth, faith will confirm the desire or the hope that is in you, so that when you speak the Word, it will manifest. Faith perceives the Word as real fact. It perceives that your body is healed as a real fact; it perceives that you have exited the land of average as a real fact; it perceives that you are the head and not the tail as a real fact. Faith in God's Word does not perceive that you are broke, busted, and disgusted. Faith is final authority in God's Word. You must have faith in God's Word, not faith in you, not in your finances, not in your possessions, and not in your job. When you have faith in God and perceive the Word as real fact and final authority, the Word coming out of your mouth must manifest. You cannot get this result from only 1 hour a week in the Word of God or from just going to church. Really open yourself to Hebrews 11:3.

Hebrews 11:3 – Amplified
By faith we understand that the worlds
[during the successive ages] were framed

(fashioned, put in order, and equipped for their intended purpose) by the word of God, so that what we see was not made out of things which are visible.

Faith does more than allow us to perceive the Word as real fact; it allows us to receive it as a confirmation. Here in Hebrews 11:3, faith also gives us the spiritual revelation of understanding. This scripture says that everything is done by the Word. The earth was framed as a result of what God spoke and things once invisible were made visible. The earth is visible as a result of a spoken Word. Said plainly, the Word did a few things — it framed, it fashioned after, and it put in order. Glory to God! God's Word is available today to put in order the things that we could not put in order on our own. It equips believers to overcome in this world, by the Word of God. (1 John 5:4)

Faith Pressure Applied

There are four results that you can expect when you apply faith pressure to the Word of God, as you speak the Word from your mouth. The Bible says in Hosea 4:6 that God's people perish for a lack of knowledge. A lack or insufficiency in any area is the result of a lack of spiritual knowledge from the Word of God. That lack of knowledge makes us unsuccessful in producing what God has already said that we could produce by believing His Word.

There are people that profess the Word, but still have the same failures, same mishaps, and same insufficiencies. This happens when confidence is not playing a part in the Word. God says that confidence (faith) in the Word comes from *hearing* the Word - not just reading it, not just fellowshipping, but by *hearing* the Word. When you apply faith pressure to God's Word, His Word will do the following four things for you:

1. Uphold. – It will uphold what it comes out to do. Whatever is based on the Word of God and spoken from your mouth, will be upheld by the Word of God. (Isaiah 55:11) (Hebrews 1:3)

2. Maintain Success. – The Word of God will maintain success. In order to maintain success, the Word has to come out of your mouth. It has to come out of your mouth consistently, to the point that you are experiencing tangible success. (III John 2)

3. Guide You. – God's Word coming out of your mouth will act as a guide for you. It will lead you into your wealthy place. (Isaiah 48:17)

4. Propel You. – God's Word coming out of your mouth will propel you and bring you into a life of peace and prosperity as you hear and obey His Word. (Deuteronomy 28:1-8)

Let's back this up with scripture…

Hebrews 1:3 – King James Version
Who being the brightness of his glory, and the express image of his person, and up-holding all things by the Word of his power, when he had by himself purged our sins, sat down on the right hand of the Majesty on high;

Hebrews 1:3 - Amplified
He is the sole expression of the glory of God [the Light-being, the out raying or radiance of the divine], and He is the perfect imprint and very image of [God's] nature, upholding and maintaining and guiding and propelling the universe by His mighty word of power. When He had by offering Himself accomplished our cleansing of sins and riddance of guilt, He sat down at the right hand of the divine Majesty on high.

Remember the Word of God does not become effective in our lives until we have confidence in what we speak, and we cannot have confidence unless we hear the Word of God. Jesus lived this principle. He knew how it worked. He depended upon what He had read, seen, and heard the Father speak. Even though He was the Son of God in the flesh, Jesus only spoke what the Father told Him to speak from the Word. By being led by the Holy Spirit, He spoke it with confidence.

Let's look at Matthew…

Matthew 4:1-4 – King James Version
Then was Jesus led up of the Spirit into the wilderness to be tempted of the devil.
And when he had fasted forty days and forty nights, he was afterward an hungered.
And when the tempter came to him, he said, If thou be the Son of God, command that these stones be made bread.
But he answered and said, It is written, Man shall not live by bread alone, but by every word that proceedeth out of the mouth of God.

It says it is written. Today, if you are going through a challenge, all you have to do is look in the Bible and realize, that *it is written.* Receive the Word into your heart, so that it can come out of your mouth with confidence. Then say boldly, "*It is written* that the just shall live by faith. *It is written* that I am the head and not the tail. *It is written* that I have the wisdom of God today. *It is written* that the Lord takes pleasure in the prosperity of His servant, therefore I receive my prosperity today."

(Psalm 35:27)

Matthew 4:4 – Amplified
But He replied, It has been written, Man shall not live and be upheld and sustained by bread alone, but by every word that comes forth from the mouth of God.

Confessions for Healing, Weakness, and Fear

Now let us put together a study sheet of the following three areas of confession: 1) healing, 2) weakness, and 3) fear. Remember that what we say is what we get; what we confess is what we possess; and our confession of the Word precedes our possession of the promises of God. (Precedes means to go before.) Before you see the manifestation of God's promises, the Word must proceed *first* out of your mouth.

1. When I need a healing - Most people do not want to confess healing scriptures until they are sick. Why not do it right now? Say, "By His stripes I am already healed. Lord, I thank you that I am already healed today, in Jesus' name." God Himself called things that be not as though they were. If you have challenges believing in this area and confessing God's Word is not working in your life, it is probably because

you are investing more of your time in the things of the world than in the things of God. Your life may be affected by doubt, because you are not hearing enough of the Word to have confidence in it. In order to have what the Word says you can have, you must apply faith pressure to the Word. He that endures to the end gets the real reward. The Word honors obedience, not slothfulness. (Deuteronomy 28:1) The Holy Spirit is always speaking to you, not to take anything from you, but to transmit something to you. Confession is not going to work unless it comes by faith, and faith is not coming (it is not transmitted to you) unless you are hearing the Word of God. The Word says in Romans 10:17 that faith cometh by hearing, and hearing by the Word of God. That means if we are not hearing the Word of God, we are not receiving faith. We cannot have faith-filled power without confidence and we cannot have power without the Word. Faith and the Word work together as co-producers. It is the same creative power that dwells in

Christ Jesus, and now is in every born-again Believer.

So when you need healing in your body, this is what you should do - go to the Bible. Find the healing scriptures, apply your faith, and believe you receive. Here is a scripture that you as a believer can manifest in your life...

I Peter 2:24- Amplified
He personally bore our sins in His [own] body on the tree [as on an altar and offered Himself on it], that we might die (cease to exist) to sin and live to righteousness. By His wounds you have been healed.

The Amplified Bible says that you have been healed, healed is past tense; it has already happened. Just continue to hold onto and rely on the Word of God. Confess the Word that says you have already been healed. Now you may be thinking, what does this mean? It means that you hold God to His Word. You go to the scripture and you say, "Lord, according to

I Peter 2:24, you said in your Word that by the stripes of Jesus I have been healed." Keep hearing it, and saying it, and saying it, and hearing it, until you have confidence in what you have been hearing and saying out of your mouth. The Bible tells us that we have been healed, so say, "Lord, I thank you that I have already been healed." Now how long do you say it? You say it at night when you are going to sleep; you say it when you get up in the morning; you say it when you are walking, and you say it when you are in your car. You say it when you do not feel like saying it, you say it when you do feel like saying it. Just keep on saying it. You cannot borrow someone else's faith. You have to say it, and say it, and say it, until you see it. Even after you see your healing and are already well, still keep saying it. "Lord, I thank you that by your stripes I am healed, I have already received my healing. I thank you for it right now in the name of Jesus. Amen."

2. When I feel weak – Before you can confess anything you have to first recognize that

something needs to change. When God moved upon the face of the waters, He saw darkness. He identified what He saw, but He did not speak it. He saw darkness, He then moved, He hovered and nothing took formation until He spoke! So what do you say when your flesh is weak, and your mind and body feel weak? Let's look at Psalm 27:1...

Psalm 27:1 – King James Version
The Lord is my light and my salvation; whom shall I fear? the Lord is the strength of my life; of whom shall I be afraid?

Say, "The Lord is <u>my</u> strength now!" Do not speak doubt, speak His Word. Do not say, "What am I going to do?" or "I do not know how things are going to work out." All of this is speaking doubt. You do not need to worry about the problem because you already have the answer; it is in your mouth. (Romans 10:8). Philippians 4:13 is a familiar scripture. Keep in mind we are laying a foundation for the power of words. That scripture says:

Philippians 4:13 – King James Version
I can do all things through Christ which
strengtheneth me.

If you continue to say, "I can do all things through Christ who strengthens me", then that means you are on your way to being strengthened. So say it. You need to realize that you are doing things in the present tense through Christ, who is strengthening you *right now.* The anointing in your life is present tense; it is operating right now when your faith is used. When you are feeling weak say, "Lord, I thank you that *I am doing all things* through Christ who is my strength today." This is how you build yourself up and gain confidence in the words that you speak.

3. When I am fearful - When fear tries to overtake you, what do you need coming out of your mouth? Go with me to Psalm 118:6.

Psalm 118:6 – King James Version
"The Lord is on my side; I will not fear:
what can man do unto me?"

You see nothing can be upheld,
maintained, superceded, or propelled
unless it is birthed from the Word of God.
The Lord is on your side and nobody can
mess with you. You have been walking
around worrying about the devil, but the
devil is defeated! In the book of Job, it
says the devil is going to and fro seeking
whom he can devour, but that was before
the Judgment. In John 16:8-11, it says:

John 16:8-11 – King James Version
"And when He is come He will reprove,
(talking about the Spirit, The Holy Ghost),
He will reprove the world of sin, and of
righteousness, and of judgment: and listen
to verse 9: Of sin, because they believe not
on me. Verses 10-11: Of righteousness,
because I go to the Father, and you see me
no more; Of judgment, because the prince
of this world is judged.

Now here's how the Amplified reads:

John 16:9-11 - Amplified
About sin, because they do not believe in
Me (trust in, rely on and adhere to Me);
verse 10:   About righteousness
(uprightness of heart and right standing
with God), because I go to My Father and
you will see Me no longer; (But listen to
this, this is what the Holy Ghost's job is)
About judgment, because the ruler or the
evil genius, the prince of this world, Satan,
is judged and condemned and sentence al-
ready is passed upon him.

Believe the good news, the Lord is on your
side. You are not in a battle fighting the
devil. He is already defeated. The
sentence against the devil is already
passed. You are experiencing the side
effects of Satan's reign when he had
authority over God's people. Think about
this - when you see a tree swaying in the
wind, it is not the wind that you see, but
the side effects of the wind. As a result of

an anointed Word coming out of your mouth, you do not have to worry about the devil anymore. His authority was taken when Jesus went to Calvary and paid a heavy price to set you free from the power of sin and death. (Romans 8:1-2) (Romans 6:14).

In II Timothy it says…

II Timothy 1:7 – King James Version
For God had not given us the spirit of fear, but of power and of love and of a sound mind.

God has given us a spirit that is calm, well balanced, disciplined, and self-controlled. When judgment took place, it gave you authority over every walking creature; over your job, your business, and over everything that involves you, including the power over words. All you have to do is believe and receive it. When you receive it confidently and you speak the Word of God, the results will be health, strength, power, wealth, prosperity, and all the things that go along with God's Word. Remember speaking the Word of God precedes experiencing the promises of God!

Chapter 2

Faith and Confession

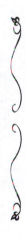

"...even God, who quickeneth the dead, and calleth those things which be not as though they were."

Romans 4:17 KJV

Chapter 2

Faith and Confession

Our Words are the Cornerstones to Our Lives

Holding Fast to Our Profession

Clarification of the Wrong Type of Confession

Confessing is Testifying to Something We Know

Chapter 2

Faith and Confession

Most people do not realize that the words they speak out of their mouths form the cornerstones to their lives. We must understand that words are used to do more than transmit information. Your words will either move towards faith or fear. As discussed in the last chapter, there are two fundamental principles about words that we have to appreciate - words are spiritual and they carry power. The Bible declares that by your words you will be justified and by your words you will be condemned. This means there is a side effect to the words that flow out of your mouth. They are either full of faith or full of fear.

Do you know that every word you speak affects your life? Even if you are not aware of this principle or are not quite sure you understand it, it is true — every word you speak does effect your life.

As you are dealing with certain issues in your life and you continue to speak about those issues, the fact that you keep speaking about those issues allows them to continue to show up in your life. The words you speak will either help promote your life or they will destroy your life. Let us look at Proverbs 11:3.

Proverbs 11:3 – King James Version
The integrity of the upright shall guide them, but the perverseness of the transgressor shall destroy them.

Proverbs 11:3 – Amplified
The integrity of the upright shall guide
them, but the willful contrariness or the
crookedness of the treacherous shall
destroy them.

In other words, those who willfully use the
Word of God contrary to its meaning – can
expect it to actually come back and destroy
them by giving birth to treachery.
Remember and acknowledge who you are
in the Anointed One and His anointing. If
the Word of God coming out of your mouth
is contrary to how Jesus had the Word
coming out of his mouth, it will destroy
you. What does Proverbs 18:21 say?

Proverbs 18:21 – King James Version
Death and life are in the power of the
tongue, and they that love it shall eat the
fruit thereof.

It says here that you control two things in
your mouth; life and death. Death is not
controlled by anything else. Death is

controlled by what is flowing out of your mouth. If you do not have the right things flowing out of your mouth, you will end up producing death. If you willfully use words contrary to the way that God intended them to be used, contrary to the image of God, which is man, they will end up destroying you.

When we talk about the power of words, we have to grab hold of the fact that words have power; and if we speak the right words, they will produce power in our lives. Go with me to Deuteronomy 30…

Deuteronomy 30:19-20 – King James Version
I call heaven and earth to record this day against you, that I have set before you life and death, blessing and cursing: therefore choose life, that both thou and thy seed may live: That thou mayest love the Lord thy God, and that thou mayest obey his voice, and that thou mayest cleave unto him: for he is thy life, and the length of thy days: that thou mayest dwell in the land which the Lord sware unto thy fathers, to Abraham, to Isaac, and to Jacob, to give them.

Say this out loud, "Life is before me, the blessing is before me, healing is before me, peace is before me, and joy is before me." The Lord says in His Word that He set these things before you, not behind you, but in front of you. He set before you peace and total life prosperity, but He also set before you death. You choose. The Word of God is saying that you have the ability to be depressed, unhealthy, unfit, envious, or fearful.

In order for you to choose life, your spoken words must be in line with the Word of God. You do this by getting your words hooked up with God's Words and then speaking only those things that God would have you say. When you have God's Words coming out of your mouth, you will cause His ability to work on your behalf and bring forth the good life. You choose the good life by loving God *first* and obeying His voice, while speaking the Words that He would have you to speak over your life day after day.

Holding Fast to Our Profession

There are (3) steps that must first be in your heart. Let's start by looking at Hebrews...

Hebrews 4:14 – King James Version
Seeing that we have a great high priest, that is passed in to the heavens, Jesus the Son of God, let us hold fast our profession.

Hebrews 4:14 - Amplified
Inasmuch then as we have a great High Priest Who has already ascended and passed through the heavens, Jesus the Son of God, let us hold fast our confession of faith in Him.

Step 1. The Word says for us to hold on to what is coming out of our mouths, hold fast to the confession of our faith. There is a reason why God wants you to do this. It is so you do not get to the point that you confess the Word of God mechanically, expecting what you say to be effective.

Mark 7:6 - Amplified

...These people [constantly] honor Me with their lips, but their hearts hold off and are far distant from Me.

Jesus said that through tradition the Pharisees and the Sadducees went forth declaring the Word of God, but through their traditions they made the Word of God non-effective. (Mark 7:13) Do not confess out of religious habit. You confess the Word by faith.

<u>Step 2</u>. It is vitally important that you get the Word in your mouth as soon as your feet hit the floor every morning, so that you can have the power of God's ability operating in your life, marriage, finances, body, home, and in everything that involves you throughout the day. You may be able to remember and quote scripture, but have yet to produce manifested results in your life. You may be saying, "Lord, by your stripes I am healed;" so where is your healing? You may be saying, "I am out of debt, my needs are met;" where's your debt

freedom? You are not receiving or possessing what you are confessing, because your confession is all in your head, not in your heart. After you have confessed consistently with your heart, then out of your mouth, you will be able to experience all of God's promises that He made to Abraham, Isaac, and Jacob. You can experience these because God gave the same promises to you. Jesus said that His Words are Spirit and life. So if His Words are Spirit and life, then they should work through you, with you, and for you, too. Hallelujah!

Step 3. This step comes from the book of James. It is referring to controlling the tongue.

James 3:5-8 – King James Version

Even so the tongue is a little member and boasteth great things. Behold how great a matter a little fire kindleth.

And the tongue is a fire, a world of iniquity: so is the tongue among our members that it defileth the whole body, and setteth on fire the course of nature and it is set on fire of hell. For every kind of beasts, and of birds, and of serpents, and of things in the sea, is tamed, and has been tamed of mankind:

But the tongue can no man tame. It is an unruly evil, full of deadly poison.

James 3:5-8 – Amplified

Even so the tongue is a little member, and it can boast great things. See how much wood or how great a forest a tiny spark can set ablaze!

And the tongue is a fire. [The tongue is a] world of wickedness set among our members, contaminating and depraving the whole body and setting on fire the wheel of birth (the cycle of man's nature), being itself ignited by hell (Gehenna).

For every kind of beast and bird, of reptile and sea animal, can be tamed and has been tamed by human genius (nature).

But the human tongue can be tamed by no man. It is a restless (undisciplined, irreconcilable) evil, full of deadly poison.

It says here, that no man can tame the tongue. In other words, with our natural ability we are not capable of controlling our tongues. It did not say, however, that an anointed vessel could not tame its tongue.

Romans 7:15 – Amplified
For I do not understand my own actions [I am baffled, bewildered]. I do not practice or accomplish what I wish, but I do the very thing that I loathe [which my moral instinct condemns].

You see, Paul said that thing that I want to do or that thing I desire to do, I do not end up doing it. Why? Because I am not controlled by the anointing, not controlled by the Spirit of God.

If you are born of God, then old things have passed away and behold all things have become new. This means you have a new controlled way of speaking, a new confident attitude, and a new faith-filled mindset. How does this happen? It happens by getting more of the Word of God in you. Once the Word of God has taken root in your heart, it can come forth out of your mouth, and produce the life that God wants you to have – The Abundant Life. (John 10:10)

__Clarification of the Wrong__
__Type of Confession__

You have to be very careful about what you confess. Here are some very common confessions people say that are wrong.

Wrong confession #1

You have heard people say, "That is unbelievable, I just can't believe that." Well the question is, why can't they believe it? We, in the body of Christ, have to remember that words are spiritual and they are powerful. The words coming out of your mouth are going to affect what you believe. Remember what the Word of God says…

Mark 9:23 – King James Version
Jesus said unto him, If thou canst believe, all things are possible to him that

believeth.

The end result may look like something that was impossible for man, but God will have made it happen anyhow. Believe it, because it is reality! (Luke 1:37)

Wrong confession #2

How many times have you heard people say that Jesus will work it out? Well, Jesus is not going to do anything else about it. He has already done it. He has already worked everything out on Calvary. He said it Himself on Calvary, "It is **finished**." He has already settled it and has given us all authority to carry out His will. So to sit around saying the Lord is going to work it out, means you have just entered into doubt and unbelief by forgetting that God has already worked it out. He is finished – It is done – finito / period!

Wrong confession #3

This is a famous one. When you hear a Christian without spiritual revelation say,

"All things work together for good", in reference to an undesirable or tragic event, you must know that that is not what the Word means – God forbid. This is the first of all unqualified statements. What the Word is saying is that your prayer time, study time, fellowship time, intercessory time, and your partnering with God's will for your life, is going to work out for your good. God's will is that you prosper as the Word says in III John.

III John 2 – Amplified

Beloved, I pray that you may prosper in every way and [that your body] may keep well, even as [I know] your soul keeps well and prospers.

Confessing is Testifying to Something We Know

Let's establish one thing, true confession is testifying to something that we know, believe, and receive as a reality from the Word. In other words, we cannot confess or witness about things we do not know. If you know something, then you can confess it with confidence. What many of us have done is make the Word of God of no effect in our life by nullifying the testimony of the Word of God. We have taken the Bible and we have it in our heads, but not enough has been deeply rooted into our hearts. That is why too many believers have not been able to see the power of God's Word work.

The following seven points will assist you in becoming more *Word-conscious*. These points will also stop you from making the Word of God non-effective in your life.

(1) Do not try to believe, just act on the Word.

Do not try to believe, just act on the Word. The Word should bring forth the manifestation of what you already believed you received. You do not have to shout, "I am a believer!" People will be able to see that you are a believer because of the fruit you bear.

Matthew 7:20 – King James Version
Wherefore by their fruits ye shall know
them.

(2) Do not have double confessions.

On one hand, you could confess, "Lord, I thank you because I am wealthy, blessed, rich and loaded, and all my needs are met." On the other hand, you could look at your current circumstances and begin to ask, "How am I going to get the money?" When you question how, you are not trusting God, therefore you enter into the realm of doubt through your words. Keep your faith in God's Word regardless of your circumstances. He will show up in the midst of your circumstance, if you do not give way to fear and doubt.

James 1:8 – Amplified
[For being as he is] a man of two minds
(hesitating, dubious, irresolute), [he is]
unstable and unreliable and uncertain

about everything [he thinks, feels, decides].

(3) Do not trust in other people's faith alone, use your own.

Faith is confidence in the Word of God. Be confident in the Word, which is planted in your heart and confessed with your mouth. Placing your trust in the faith of others alone is equivalent to borrowing somebody else's faith for something that God has told you to do. I once heard a wise man say, "You can only live on borrowed wings for so long". That person's faith works for them; it is not yours, it does not belong to you. The Word says, for YOU to have faith in God, not in someone else. You must *personally* have faith in God, in order for the Word that is coming out of your mouth to work for you.

(4) Do your own believing.

Do your own believing and confessing. Do not sit around asking every Christian you see to believe God for you. They can

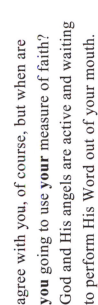

agree with you, of course, but when are **you** going to use **your** measure of faith? God and His angels are active and waiting to perform His Word out of your mouth.

Psalm 103:20 – Amplified

Bless (affectionately, gratefully praise) the Lord, you His angels, you mighty ones who do His commandments, hearkening to the voice of His word.

(5) Do not speak doubt or unbelief.

Avoid having conversations with those that want to sit around all day talking doubt. In Genesis 1, it says that darkness was upon the face of the deep. You may have imagined a big giant dark cloud. That is not what that was. There was a lot of sin present. Sin is separation from God, which God considers to be darkness. Anything that is separated from God operates in darkness. God looked upon the face of the deep and said, "Let there be light."

You must speak only those things you want to see in your life. When you are in a situation where darkness is present, maybe in your finances, marriage, or an issue with your children, and there seems to be no way out; avoid speaking doubt and unbelief. Do not do it. Open up your mouth and declare God's prosperity over your life. Make the Word of God your final authority.

(6) Do not meditate on sickness or disease. If your body is sick, do not look at that situation as being sick and afflicted. Just keep saying "Lord I thank You, by Your stripes I'm healed. I have already received my healing, in Jesus' name. Amen." You are already healed because Jesus said so. That is the final authority – that is His Word!

(7) Never consider failure. You can never find the answer inside a problem. You find your answer inside the Word. The Word provides the answers to life. You need to get the Word before you, get it in your ears, get it on your tongue,

and get it coming out of your mouth. Once it is built up inside of you and you speak it, you will then be able to experience the benefits, and failure won't be an option. Now that we have looked at the things we do not want to do, let's look at the things we should do to get the Word to work for us. In Jeremiah 1:12, in the Amplified Bible, God says, "I am alert and active, watching over my Word to perform it." God is saying that if you have His Word, He is active in *waiting* to perform it. Everything that you are believing God for, the best for your children, your family, and your life, all of that fruit will come forth out of the Word, from your heart, by your mouth. God is waiting for His Word to come out of your mouth. His desire is not to wait until you get home or to your next job interview to bless you. He is waiting for you to open your mouth now! Just speak the Word, because He is active to perform it.

In the book of Psalms chapter 103:20 we

read that the angels of God hearken unto the commandment of God. In other words, they hearken unto the voice of God; they are waiting for you to speak in order for God's Word to become active, then they can help bring it to pass. It is vitally important that you understand the proper steps to speaking the Word of God out of your mouth, so that you will be able to see and experience the promises of God.

Here are the proper steps to apply the Word of God:

Remind God of His Word.
God instructs us to remind Him of His Word. The important question here is: Do you know His Word in order to be able to remind Him of it? In the book of Isaiah 43...

Isaiah 43:26 – Message Translation
So, make your case against me. Let's have this out. Make your arguments. Prove you're in the right.

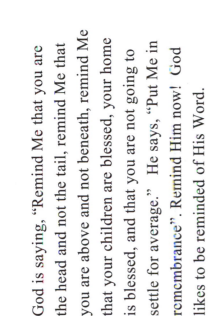

God is saying, "Remind Me that you are the head and not the tail, remind Me that you are above and not beneath, remind Me that your children are blessed, your home is blessed, and that you are not going to settle for average." He says, "Put Me in remembrance". Remind Him now! God likes to be reminded of His Word.

Believe that the Lord confirms the Word of His servant.

In Isaiah 44, it says…

Isaiah 44:26 – King James Version
That confirmeth the word of his servant, and performeth the counsel of his messengers…

Isaiah 44:26 – Message Translation
He backs the word of His servants…

In other words, it is the Lord who confirms the Word of His servant. It is the Lord that is going to confirm your prosperity, not you. It is not your ability alone that is going to make it happen. It is His ability, which is His super, upon your natural ability, creating supernatural ability to make things happen.

I John 2:20 – King James Version
But ye have an unction from the Holy One, and ye know all things.

Remember the Word of God stands forever.

In Isaiah chapter 40, it says that the Word of God stands forever.

Isaiah 40:8 – King James Version
The grass withereth, the flower fadeth; but the word of our God shall stand forever.

Know, God's Word does not return void.

In Isaiah chapter 55, it says…

Isaiah 55:10-11 – King James Version
For as the rain cometh down, and the snow from heaven, and returneth not thither, but watereth the earth, and maketh it bring

forth and bud, that it may give seed to the sower, and bread to the eater:

So shall my word be that goeth forth out of my mouth, it shall not return to me void, but it shall accomplish that which I please, and it shall prosper in the thing whereto I sent it.

God is reminding us that the snow and the rain come down, but they do not return. He compares this to His Word. He says, so shall it be that my Word that goes forth out of my mouth shall not return void. He adds that His word shall *produce* and *prosper*.

Chapter 3

Operating in God's Ability

"… because He Who lives in you is greater (mightier) that he who is the world."

I John 4:4 AMPLIFIED

Chapter 3

Operating in God's Ability

Releasing God's Ability in Your Life

Questions that You must Answer
to have God's Ability Released

C h a p t e r 3

Operating in God's Ability

There are four steps that you need to know concerning God's power flowing out of your mouth. Through your faith confession you are hooked up to God's supernatural ability. This will allow you to ultimately produce what God says in His Word, in your life. In the book of Genesis, it says....

Genesis 1:1-4 – King James Version
In the beginning God created the heaven

and the earth.
And the earth was without form, and void;
and darkness was upon the face of the
deep. And the spirit of God moved upon
the face of the waters.
And God said, Let there be light:
and there was light.
And God saw the light, that it was good:
and God divided the light from the darkness.

It says, "…the earth was without form", the earth was without form…the earth was without form. Now let's take your body — your healing was without form, **are you getting this**? Your bank account was without form. Your marriage was without form. Everything was without form, and void, and nothing was there. Notice in the scriptures that even though darkness was evident, and the weapon was already present, none of those circumstances had authority over the spoken Word of God.

You may be dealing with a certain area in

your life today where it is evident that a weapon against you has formed. Even though it is there and is hovering, it does not take precedence over the spoken Word of God. (Isaiah 54:17) Remember this, in Genesis 1, God saw… the void and the earth not yet formed, and darkness (chaos/sin) upon the face of the deep. He still had the ability to walk in that presence, look around, and call things that be not as though they were. He changed what had existed before, into what He wanted to see by the Words that He spoke. Glory!

Romans 4:17 – King James Version
…even God, who quickeneth the dead, and calleth those things which be not as though they were.

Likewise, you must imitate God and identify any insufficiencies in your life, and then call those things that be not as though they were. Change what you see by what you say. You are made in His image and in His likeness. What He did, you can do also. Change it! God said it, and then He saw it, so you say it and then you will see it, as long as you obey the Word that God speaks!

Step #1 – Conception

The Word must be conceived in your heart, not in your head. You must be able to see through your spiritual eyes and not your natural eyes. This is how God was able to call those things that be not as though they were. He saw them through spiritual eyes and spoke what He wanted to see as though they already were. God cannot just start something without finishing it first. He always begins with the end in mind.

For example, you may be saying, "Oh Lord Jesus, I thank you that by your Spirit I am going to be ok soon!" Well, that is your desire, but that is not what the Word says to do. The Word says call things that be not as though "they were", as if it already "is." If it is wholeness, then say, "Lord, I thank you that I am already made whole!"

Are you listening? Then say this aloud, "I am already full of peace and joy."

The Word of God conceived in your heart is key. The Word of God that you are standing on, holding onto, and believing in must become real to you.   Once it becomes real to you, you will speak out of your mouth what you believe. The Word says from the abundance of the heart the mouth speaks. (Matthew 12:34) This means that whatever is in your heart in abundance will come out of your mouth. If you only have head knowledge, then you are only going to operate by what you see. If the Word is in your heart in abundance, then you are going to operate by faith, meaning you will operate by what you do not see. The Word says for we walk by faith and not by sight. (II Corinthians 5:7) In order to get the Word in your heart, so that conception can take place, you have to sow the Word into your spirit, by hearing the Word of God. Once it is conceived in your heart, like a seed sown into the ground, you will speak it and eventually it will give manifested birth to the Word of God. Go to I Corinthians...

I Corinthians 2:14 – King James Version
"But the natural man receiveth not the things of the Spirit of God: for they are foolishness unto him: neither can he know them, because they are spiritually discerned."

I Corinthians 2:14 – Amplified
But the natural, non-spiritual man does not accept or welcome or admit into his heart the gifts and teachings and revelations of the Spirit of God, for they are folly (meaningless nonsense) to him; and he is incapable of knowing them (of progressively recognizing, understanding, and becoming better acquainted with them) because they are spiritually discerned and estimated and appreciated.

God's will is for everyone to be healed, whole, and set free from any bondage, but the natural or non-spiritual man does not accept God's way of doing things. You see, your circumstances in the natural should not dictate what is in your heart. If the Word of God is not in your heart, then your circumstances will dictate your life. Let me tell you something about circumstances. They are limited. They will always change in favor of a believer that speaks God's Word. When you get the Word of God coming out of your mouth, it will not return void. It always performs what it is sent out to do. God is always active to make sure all undesirable circumstances change in the lives of His children.

When you depend upon God's Word to give you joy, your circumstances will change. You will be changed because God is within you, the Hope of Glory! Even though your current circumstances may have you walking through the valley of the shadow of death, the Word says that you do not have to fear because God is with you. (Psalm 23:4) So all of Who He is is with you every time you walk through the valley. It does not matter what you are seeing, it will not harm you, it is only a shadow. Keep your mouth focused on the Word of God and what He says about your circumstances. Say what God says in His Word until it comes to pass.

Remember in I Corinthians 2:14 that the natural man, the non-spiritual man, does not accept or welcome God's Word in His life. He does not receive the gifts and the teachings and the revelations of the Spirit of God. Why? Because the Word says that they are meaningless nonsense to him.

Step #2 – Formation

Step number #1 declares that first, the Word must be conceived in your heart. Step #2 declares that the Word must be formed on your tongue. The Word says that death and life are in the power of the tongue, and until you conceive it in your heart, you cannot get it out of your mouth. Paul declares in Romans 10 that the Word that he preached is in our mouths. Let's take a look...

Romans 10:8 – King James Version
But what saith it? The word is nigh thee, even in thy mouth, and in thy heart: that is, the word of faith, which we preach;

The Word of God is near you. Glory to God! Demons in hell have the Word all around them. They know the Word and they tremble, but they do not have the authority to use it. You and I walk around blessed and redeemed of the Lord. Listen, the Word is near you, right now. You have the authority to open the Bible, read it aloud, get it in your ear-gate so that it may be sown into your heart, formed on your tongue and declared boldly out of your mouth. Notice, Paul classified it as being located in two different areas: 1) in your mouth and 2) in your heart. He says that as a result of it being in the heart and in the mouth, you can call the Word to action by your faith in God.

Step #3 – Vocalization

You have conceived the Word in your heart and formed it on your tongue. Step #3 requires the Word be spoken out of your mouth. Three things have to take place in order to release God's ability and proper direction in your life: <u>conception, formation</u>, and <u>vocalization</u> of the Word of God. If you do not conceive it, then you cannot form it, and certainly you will not be able to speak it. Let us go to Romans 10...

Romans 10:9 – King James Version
That if thou shalt confess with thy mouth the Lord Jesus, and shalt believe in thine heart that God raised him from the dead, thou shalt be saved.

Here in Romans 10:9 it explains why the Power of Words is so vitally important – your salvation hangs on this spiritual law. For with the heart, which is the soul (the mind, will, and emotions) of man, he believes. So as the Word is conceived in the heart of a man, he begins to believe. He then can confess the Word with his mouth and salvation will come. Amen. Glory be to God!

Step #4 – Faith with Action

Let's recap…Step #1 the Word is conceived, Step #2 you formed the Word on your tongue, Step #3 you speak the Word out of your mouth, and now Step #4 you put your faith into action. You have to expect what it is that you are declaring. The Word coming out of your mouth has power, but without works of obedience it is dead. Let's take a look at the following scriptures…

James 2:17 – Amplified
So also faith, if it does not have works (deeds and actions of obedience to back it up), by itself is destitute of power (inoperative, dead).

John 6:63 – King James Version
It is the spirit that quickeneth; the flesh

profiteth nothing: the words that I speak unto you, they are spirit, and they are life.

Flesh profits nothing...
Jesus says the spirit quickeneth and the flesh profits nothing and the Words that He speaks are spirit and life. He says that there is no benefit whatsoever, or no profit in the flesh. This means that there is no profit in your sensible thinking and your reasoning. You must be ready to speak as God speaks to you. You must <u>also</u> be ready to hear and obey after you have received the Word.

<u>Questions You must Answer</u>

The following are four questions you need to ask yourself regarding God's ability being released on your life:

1. Do I want God's ability released on my life? You should think about that. Jesus said, "On earth as it is in heaven". If you need it in heaven, you need to have it down here as well... "On earth as it is in

heaven". Well, let me ask you a question – What's in heaven? Joy, peace, prosperity, wealth and everything else good you cannot even imagine.

Mathew 6:10 – Amplified
Your kingdom come, Your will be done on earth as it is in heaven.

2. <u>Do I have the right purpose in my heart, to have His ability released on my life?</u>
God is not going to give it to you just because you want it. Consider a 10-year old child that wants to do everything he sees you do. If he asks to drive the car, would you hand him the keys? No. You may let him touch the steering wheel and sit on your lap while you drive about ten feet, but you would not just give him the keys. Why not? He is your child, your flesh and blood. He has everything that belongs to you; he is a part of your household; he has everything. Why don't you release the car to him? You know why. It is because you cannot trust him with it right now.

He is not yet responsible or developed enough to handle it. So why should God allow you to walk around, wealthy, blessed, healthy, and with everything that is in His Word, and you have not yet proved that you are responsible. You may have the wrong purpose in your heart. Are you seeing this? It might be something from your past, it might be something about how you see your future, it could be anything, but something can clog up the windows of heaven over your life. The only way to get the windows of heaven opened over your life is by hearing and obeying the Word of God. (Malachi 3:10) Keep in mind that without faith it is impossible to please God, and God rewards those who diligently seek Him. (Hebrews 11:6) Remember you cannot have faith without hearing the Word of God, and you cannot have the Word of God formed on your tongue unless you have conceived it in your heart.

3. Do I want to make my way prosperous?

Of course, you want to make your way prosperous. If you have ever declared at any given time, "Lord, I thank you, I am the head, and not the tail." Then what you have said is "Lord, I want to make my way prosperous." God told Joshua that the key to bringing a prosperous life to pass was by meditating on the Word.

Joshua 1:8 – Amplified

This Book of the Law shall not depart out of your mouth, but you shall meditate on it day and night, that you may observe and do according to all that is written in it.

For then you shall make your way prosperous, and then you shall deal wisely and have good success.

4. Do I see God's method in His Word to release His ability on my life? Remember the words that you speak have power. They should be more important to you than anything else, because your words will affect your life. If you speak depression,

eventually you will experience depression; if you speak words of defeat, likewise you will experience defeat. If you are not satisfied with your current situation in life, change the words that you are speaking and begin to say what God says about your life.

Mark 11:23 – King James Version
For verily I say unto you, That whosoever shall say unto this mountain, Be thou removed, and be thou cast into the sea; and shall not doubt in his heart, but shall believe that those things which he saith shall come to pass; he shall have whatsoever he saith.

Mark 11:23 – Amplified
Truly I tell you, whoever says to this mountain, Be lifted up and thrown into the sea! and does not doubt at all in his heart but believes that <u>what he says</u> will take place, it <u>will be done for him.</u>

Jesus is saying that He spoke only the Words that the Father told Him to speak.

This is how He operated by such great faith. He allowed the anointed Word to be final authority, not the circumstances He faced.

Chapter 4

Producing Fruit

"I am the vine, ye are the branches: he that abideth in me, and I in him, the same bringeth forth much fruit ..."

St John 15:5 KJV

Chapter 4

Producing Fruit

Conditions in Your Confession to Produce the Right

Kind of Fruit

☙

Maintaining and Holding on to the Power of Words

by Your Confession

☙

Seven Conditions You Must Meet in Order to See

God's Blessings Flow in Your Life

~96~

Chapter 4

Producing Fruit

There are conditions to your confession, which you need to understand. One important element to learn is that the Word of God flowing through a willing vessel determines the quality of fruit produced. In other words, when you hear the Word of God, faith comes to you. You need to have confidence in what you are hearing from the Word so you can respond to it. When you hear the Word of God you can submit to it, but still not be obedient to it.

Obedience must play a role in order to produce the right kind of fruit. Hearing and believing, without demonstrative actions of obedience, will not produce the fruit you desire. In Mark 7, Jesus says...

Mark 7:13 – King James Version
Making the word of God none effective through your traditions, which ye have delivered: and many such like things do ye.

Mark 7:13 – Amplified Bible
Thus you are nullifying and making void and of no effect [the authority of] the Word of God through your tradition, which you [in turn] hand on. And many things of this kind you are doing.

Simply put, the Word of God has been made non-effective because of something that you have done. The word mentions "things", meaning more than one. There is more than one "thing" that you have been doing that has stopped the promises of God from manifesting in your life.

For instance – "worry" – you deal with "worry" and then you go and share your worry with others. You may worry one minute and then turn around the next minute and say, "Oh Lord, I cast my care upon You, because You care for me." This is just one example of what has been done through tradition. You have learned to worry as a result of tradition, to the point where worrying becomes a part of your makeup. Worry and care are fear based and will not produce good fruit. If you want to produce good fruit that will last, cast your worry and care on Him once and for all, for He cares for you. (I Peter 5:7)

In a marriage, where there is no communication between a husband and a wife, the relationship becomes mechanical. Although they share the same closet space, they are just co-existing. The same thing could happen to your relationship with God. If you have the Word of God in your head and you are declaring it, but not seeing the fruit of it, your relationship is a mechanical relationship. For example, if your Pastor says, "Praise the Lord", you respond by praising the Lord. But at home, all week long, you may never praise the Lord. God is evaluating His relationship with you. Your relationship may not bear fruit because of this mindset.

Maintaining and Holding

In the book of Hebrews chapter 4, it says that the Word being mixed with faith has the ability to profit you. Now keep in mind that faith cometh by hearing and hearing by the Word of God.

Hebrews 4:2 – King James Version
For unto us was the gospel preached, as well as unto them: but the word preached did not profit them, not being mixed with faith in them that heard it.

This is saying that the Word of God will profit you if it is mixed with faith. Profit is not just dealing with money. It would be incomplete to think that way. Profit in its completeness deals with your money, body, job, home, family, marriage, and every area of your life. The Amplified says it this way.

Hebrews 4:2 – Amplified Bible

For indeed we have the glad tidings of the gospel of God proclaimed to us just as truly as the Israelites of old when the good news of deliverance from bondage came to them...

The Israelites received the good news. They heard it, but it did not benefit them. Why not? Because it was not mixed with faith. Their thinking was not fully persuaded by the promises of God. You, on the other hand, being Abraham's seed and an heir according to the promise, should be fully persuaded by the operating power of God's Word. (Proverbs 3:5,6) In order to profit in every area of your life, you have to trust God completely with your entire personality, while remaining positioned to move when the Holy Spirit prompts you to speak the Word out of your mouth.

Galatians 3:29 – King James Version
And if ye be Christ's, then are ye
Abraham's seed, and heirs according to
the promise.

Romans 4:21 – Amplified Bible
Fully satisfied and assured that God was
able and mighty to keep His word and to
do what He had promised.

Seven Conditions You Must Meet in Order to see God's Blessings Flow in Your Life

(1) Have faith in God

This is the first condition you have to meet. You must have faith in God. He is your source. You cannot have faith in your job, your own ability, or anything other than God. You cannot even have faith in your spouse. You are obligated to your spouse, but you are responsible to God. Make sure your faith is in God. (Mark 11:22)

(2) Speak to your mountains

You have to be willing to say something to your mountains. Your mountains might be your finances, your body, your home, your job, or your business. You have to speak to them and speak to them directly with Godly boldness. (Mark 11:23)

(3) Do not doubt

You cannot doubt. Doubt will cancel out what you believe. Your faith in God cannot work when doubt is present. So starve your doubts and cast those thoughts out by speaking the Word of God. (Mark 11:24)

(4) Have confidence

Have confidence in the Word of God as you confess it with your mouth. Believe in your heart that what you say will come to pass. (Hebrews 10:35) The Word of God says in the book of Joshua chapter 1, to be strong and of good courage…

Joshua 1:9 – King James Version
Have not I commanded thee? Be strong

and of a good courage; be not afraid, neither be thou dismayed: for the Lord thy God is with thee whithersoever thou goest.

Confidence is the key to manifested faith. You have to have confidence in order to produce the things for which you hope. Suppose God asks, "Do you have confidence in My Word?" "If you believe what My Word says, then your actions should line up. If your actions do not line up, then you do not believe." You say you believe... "Then show Me your confidence and I will show you My Glory!"

(5) <u>Believe you receive when you pray</u> Believe you receive what you desire at the time that you pray. Believe it right now, not 10 minutes from now. Have you ever prayed for something and it never showed up? This is because you were waiting to see it before you believed it. The world says that <u>seeing</u> is <u>believing</u>. The Word says believe you received. (Mark 11:24)

(6) <u>Say only what you believe</u>

Do not speak words that are contrary to what you believe. Do not speak what you see with your eyes, speak only the words that will produce what you believe with all your heart to receive.

Proverbs 23:7 – King James Version
For as he thinketh in his heart, so is he....

(7) <u>Forgive</u>

Forgive everyone. Do not expect God to pour out His promises on you, while you are harboring unforgiveness in your heart.

Colossians 3:13 – Amplified
Be gentle and forbearing with one another and, if one has a difference (a grievance or complaint) against another, readily pardoning each other; even as the Lord has [freely] forgiven you, so must you also [forgive].

Let's look at some scriptures to support the seven conditions.

Mark 11:22- King James Version
And Jesus answering saith unto them,
Have faith in God.

You have to have faith in God. The word does not say have faith in prayer or faith in study time. It says have faith in God. It did not even say have faith in the preacher. The preacher's responsibility does not include getting you into heaven. The preacher's responsibility is opening the Word of God and getting divine revelation to you, so you can get yourself into heaven.

Mark 11:23- King James Version
For verily I say unto you, That whosoever shall say unto this mountain, Be thou removed, and be thou cast into the sea; and shall not doubt in his heart, but shall believe that those things which he saith shall come to pass; he shall have whatsoever he saith.

Question – Are you the whosoever to

whom He is referring? It says, "Whosoever shall say unto this mountain be thou removed and be cast into the sea", and do what? "And shall not doubt in his heart" (heart = mind, will, and emotions)… And shall not doubt in his heart and shall believe those things which he has said shall come to pass, he shall have it. It does not say might have it, but shall have whatsoever he saith.

Whatever you are saying, you are going to end up seeing. Are you receiving this so far? In the beginning God said, and God said, and God said, and God said, and God said, and God saw. You are like Him because you are made in His image and in His likeness. Whatever you are looking at in your life, you said it and then it showed up. Look around…Do you like what you see? If you do not like what you are seeing, start saying something different; and line it up with the Word of God. If you are not saying anything, then you are not changing anything.

Mark 11:24- King James Version

Therefore I say unto you, What things so-ever ye desire, when ye pray, believe that ye receive them, and ye shall have them.

It says believe that you receive when you pray. Why? So you can have the things you so desire. Say aloud, "I have what I desire." Say, "I have prosperity now." Now all you have to do is believe. Now say, "I have health and healing in my bones now." Believe it. Say, "Wholeness is in my home, I have it now."

Mark 11:25- King James Version

And when ye stand praying, forgive, if ye have aught against any: that your Father also which is in heaven may forgive you your trespasses.

In this verse he says that you should forgive. Why would you expect God's Word to be activated in your life, if you are walking around in unforgiveness? God will always look at the intent of your heart, because the issues of life flow out of the abundance of the heart.

Proverbs 4:23 – King James Version
Keep thy heart with all diligence; for out of it are the issues of life.

Proverbs 4:23 – Amplified
Keep and guard your heart with all vigilance and above all that you guard, for out of it flow the springs of life.

If there is any unforgiveness in your heart, how is He going to allow your mountain to be moved? He cannot do it, if you are operating in unforgiveness. You must forgive in order to be forgiven.

The words that come from your mouth have power. Be cognizant – conscientious – aware – respectful of this truth. You will be able to direct your words in such a way that you will make your way prosperous and you will have good success. Then you surely shall see the blessing of the Lord God permeating every facet of your life in abundance. For in the book of Proverbs, it says...

Proverbs 10:22 – King James Version
The blessing of the Lord, it maketh rich,
and he addeth no sorrow with it.

Remember to always:

Have faith in God.

Speak to your mountains.

DO NOT DOUBT.

Have confidence in the words that you speak.

Believe you receive what you desire, when you pray.

Say only what you believe.

Forgive others.

About the Author

Mark A. Thomas is the founder and Pastor of My Father's House Church International of Corona, California. Formerly, a senior business executive in corporate America, Pastor Thomas received the vision of the ministry in 1993 while heading a youth outreach program in Southern California. In 1996, God instructed him audibly to preach the Word of God to the world. As such, many have been set free and restored. Mark A. Thomas & MFHCI are being used by God to inform, instruct, and teach His people how to overcome trials in this life. The foundation of the ministry is teaching the Word of God with simplicity, so new believers can understand and act upon God's Word. This is the cornerstone upon which this ministry is based. Mark not only encourages new believers, he equips them. He ministers God's principles of covenant worldwide and has been a guest on both DayStar Television Network and the Trinity Broadcasting Network.

Today, Mark A. Thomas and his helpmate, Kim reside in Corona, CA. They have three children.

Notes

Notes

Notes

Notes

Notes

Notes